# LESSON *Planner*

SUBJECT / COURSE:

TOPIC:

DATE:

GOAL:

LESSON DURATION:

| LESSON OBJECTIVES |
|---|
|  |

| SUMMARY OF TASKS / ACTION PLAN | MATERIALS / EQUIPMENT |
|---|---|
|  | |
| | **REFERENCES** |
| | |
| | **HOME WORK / TASKS** |
| | |
| | **FEEDBACK** |
| | |

# LESSON *Planner*

SUBJECT / COURSE:

TOPIC:                                          DATE:

GOAL:                                           LESSON DURATION:

| LESSON OBJECTIVES |
| --- |
|  |

| SUMMARY OF TASKS / ACTION PLAN |
| --- |
|  |

| MATERIALS / EQUIPMENT |
| --- |
|  |

| REFERENCES |
| --- |
|  |

| HOME WORK / TASKS |
| --- |
|  |

| FEEDBACK |
| --- |
|  |

# LESSON *Planner*

SUBJECT / COURSE:

TOPIC:                                                    DATE:

GOAL:                                                     LESSON DURATION:

| LESSON OBJECTIVES |
| --- |
|  |

| SUMMARY OF TASKS / ACTION PLAN |
| --- |
|  |

| MATERIALS / EQUIPMENT |
| --- |
|  |

| REFERENCES |
| --- |
|  |

| HOME WORK / TASKS |
| --- |
|  |

| FEEDBACK |
| --- |
|  |

# LESSON *Planner*

SUBJECT / COURSE:

TOPIC:                                        DATE:

GOAL:                                         LESSON DURATION:

| LESSON OBJECTIVES |
|---|
|  |

| SUMMARY OF TASKS / ACTION PLAN |
|---|
|  |

| MATERIALS / EQUIPMENT |
|---|
|  |

| REFERENCES |
|---|
|  |

| HOME WORK / TASKS |
|---|
|  |

| FEEDBACK |
|---|
|  |

# LESSON *Planner*

SUBJECT / COURSE:

TOPIC:

GOAL:

DATE:

LESSON DURATION:

| LESSON OBJECTIVES |
| --- |
|  |

| SUMMARY OF TASKS / ACTION PLAN |
| --- |
|  |

| MATERIALS / EQUIPMENT |
| --- |
|  |

| REFERENCES |
| --- |
|  |

| HOME WORK / TASKS |
| --- |
|  |

| FEEDBACK |
| --- |
|  |

# LESSON *Planner*

SUBJECT / COURSE:

TOPIC:

GOAL:

DATE:

LESSON DURATION:

| LESSON OBJECTIVES |
|---|
|  |

| SUMMARY OF TASKS / ACTION PLAN |
|---|
|  |

| MATERIALS / EQUIPMENT |
|---|
|  |

| REFERENCES |
|---|
|  |

| HOME WORK / TASKS |
|---|
|  |

| FEEDBACK |
|---|
|  |

# LESSON *Planner*

SUBJECT / COURSE:

TOPIC:                                          DATE:

GOAL:                                           LESSON DURATION:

| LESSON OBJECTIVES |
| --- |
|  |

| SUMMARY OF TASKS / ACTION PLAN | MATERIALS / EQUIPMENT |
| --- | --- |
|  |  |
|  | **REFERENCES** |
|  |  |
|  | **HOME WORK / TASKS** |
|  |  |
|  | **FEEDBACK** |
|  |  |

# LESSON *Planner*

SUBJECT / COURSE:

TOPIC:

DATE:

GOAL:

LESSON DURATION:

| LESSON OBJECTIVES |
|---|
|  |

| SUMMARY OF TASKS / ACTION PLAN |
|---|
|  |

| MATERIALS / EQUIPMENT |
|---|
|  |

| REFERENCES |
|---|
|  |

| HOME WORK / TASKS |
|---|
|  |

| FEEDBACK |
|---|
|  |

# LESSON *Planner*

SUBJECT / COURSE:

TOPIC:                                          DATE:

GOAL:                                           LESSON DURATION:

| LESSON OBJECTIVES |
|---|
|  |

| SUMMARY OF TASKS / ACTION PLAN |
|---|
|  |

| MATERIALS / EQUIPMENT |
|---|
|  |

| REFERENCES |
|---|
|  |

| HOME WORK / TASKS |
|---|
|  |

| FEEDBACK |
|---|
|  |

# LESSON *Planner*

SUBJECT / COURSE:

TOPIC:                                    DATE:

GOAL:                                     LESSON DURATION:

| LESSON OBJECTIVES |
| --- |
|  |

| SUMMARY OF TASKS / ACTION PLAN |
| --- |
|  |

| MATERIALS / EQUIPMENT |
| --- |
|  |

| REFERENCES |
| --- |
|  |

| HOME WORK / TASKS |
| --- |
|  |

| FEEDBACK |
| --- |
|  |

# LESSON *Planner*

SUBJECT / COURSE:

TOPIC:                                          DATE:

GOAL:                                           LESSON DURATION:

| LESSON OBJECTIVES |
| --- |
|  |

| SUMMARY OF TASKS / ACTION PLAN |
| --- |
|  |

| MATERIALS / EQUIPMENT |
| --- |
|  |

| REFERENCES |
| --- |
|  |

| HOME WORK / TASKS |
| --- |
|  |

| FEEDBACK |
| --- |
|  |

# LESSON *Planner*

SUBJECT / COURSE:

TOPIC:                                              DATE:

GOAL:                                               LESSON DURATION:

| LESSON OBJECTIVES |
| --- |
| |

| SUMMARY OF TASKS / ACTION PLAN | MATERIALS / EQUIPMENT |
| --- | --- |
| | |

**REFERENCES**

**HOME WORK / TASKS**

**FEEDBACK**

# LESSON *Planner*

SUBJECT / COURSE:

TOPIC:                                              DATE:

GOAL:                                               LESSON DURATION:

| LESSON OBJECTIVES |
|---|
|  |

| SUMMARY OF TASKS / ACTION PLAN |
|---|
|  |

| MATERIALS / EQUIPMENT |
|---|
|  |

| REFERENCES |
|---|
|  |

| HOME WORK / TASKS |
|---|
|  |

| FEEDBACK |
|---|
|  |

# LESSON *Planner*

SUBJECT / COURSE:

TOPIC:                                              DATE:

GOAL:                                               LESSON DURATION:

| LESSON OBJECTIVES |
|---|
|  |

| SUMMARY OF TASKS / ACTION PLAN |
|---|
|  |

| MATERIALS / EQUIPMENT |
|---|
|  |

| REFERENCES |
|---|
|  |

| HOME WORK / TASKS |
|---|
|  |

| FEEDBACK |
|---|
|  |

# LESSON *Planner*

SUBJECT / COURSE:

TOPIC:                                              DATE:

GOAL:                                               LESSON DURATION:

| LESSON OBJECTIVES |
| --- |
|  |

| SUMMARY OF TASKS / ACTION PLAN | MATERIALS / EQUIPMENT |
| --- | --- |
|  |  |
|  | **REFERENCES** |
|  |  |
|  | **HOME WORK / TASKS** |
|  |  |
|  | **FEEDBACK** |
|  |  |

# LESSON *Planner*

SUBJECT / COURSE:

TOPIC:

GOAL:

DATE:

LESSON DURATION:

| LESSON OBJECTIVES |
| --- |
|  |

| SUMMARY OF TASKS / ACTION PLAN |
| --- |
|  |

| MATERIALS / EQUIPMENT |
| --- |
|  |

| REFERENCES |
| --- |
|  |

| HOME WORK / TASKS |
| --- |
|  |

| FEEDBACK |
| --- |
|  |

# LESSON *Planner*

SUBJECT / COURSE:

TOPIC:

DATE:

GOAL:

LESSON DURATION:

| LESSON OBJECTIVES |
| --- |
| |

| SUMMARY OF TASKS / ACTION PLAN |
| --- |
| |

| MATERIALS / EQUIPMENT |
| --- |
| |

| REFERENCES |
| --- |
| |

| HOME WORK / TASKS |
| --- |
| |

| FEEDBACK |
| --- |
| |

# LESSON *Planner*

SUBJECT / COURSE:

TOPIC:                                          DATE:

GOAL:                                           LESSON DURATION:

| LESSON OBJECTIVES |
| --- |
|  |

| SUMMARY OF TASKS / ACTION PLAN |
| --- |
|  |

| MATERIALS / EQUIPMENT |
| --- |
|  |

| REFERENCES |
| --- |
|  |

| HOME WORK / TASKS |
| --- |
|  |

| FEEDBACK |
| --- |
|  |

# LESSON *Planner*

SUBJECT / COURSE:

TOPIC:

GOAL:

DATE:

LESSON DURATION:

## LESSON OBJECTIVES

## SUMMARY OF TASKS / ACTION PLAN

## MATERIALS / EQUIPMENT

## REFERENCES

## HOME WORK / TASKS

## FEEDBACK

# LESSON *Planner*

SUBJECT / COURSE:

TOPIC:

GOAL:

DATE:

LESSON DURATION:

## LESSON OBJECTIVES

## SUMMARY OF TASKS / ACTION PLAN

## MATERIALS / EQUIPMENT

## REFERENCES

## HOME WORK / TASKS

## FEEDBACK

# LESSON *Planner*

SUBJECT / COURSE:

TOPIC:                                           DATE:

GOAL:                                            LESSON DURATION:

| LESSON OBJECTIVES |
| --- |
|  |

| SUMMARY OF TASKS / ACTION PLAN |
| --- |
|  |

| MATERIALS / EQUIPMENT |
| --- |
|  |

| REFERENCES |
| --- |
|  |

| HOME WORK / TASKS |
| --- |
|  |

| FEEDBACK |
| --- |
|  |

# LESSON *Planner*

SUBJECT / COURSE:

TOPIC:                                          DATE:

GOAL:                                           LESSON DURATION:

| LESSON OBJECTIVES |
|---|
|  |

| SUMMARY OF TASKS / ACTION PLAN |
|---|
|  |

| MATERIALS / EQUIPMENT |
|---|
|  |

| REFERENCES |
|---|
|  |

| HOME WORK / TASKS |
|---|
|  |

| FEEDBACK |
|---|
|  |

# LESSON *Planner*

SUBJECT / COURSE:

TOPIC:                                   DATE:

GOAL:                                      LESSON DURATION:

| LESSON OBJECTIVES |
| --- |
|  |

| SUMMARY OF TASKS / ACTION PLAN |
| --- |
|  |

| MATERIALS / EQUIPMENT |
| --- |
|  |

| REFERENCES |
| --- |
|  |

| HOME WORK / TASKS |
| --- |
|  |

| FEEDBACK |
| --- |
|  |

# LESSON *Planner*

SUBJECT / COURSE:

TOPIC:                                          DATE:

GOAL:                                           LESSON DURATION:

| LESSON OBJECTIVES |
| --- |
| |

| SUMMARY OF TASKS / ACTION PLAN |
| --- |
| |

| MATERIALS / EQUIPMENT |
| --- |
| |

| REFERENCES |
| --- |
| |

| HOME WORK / TASKS |
| --- |
| |

| FEEDBACK |
| --- |
| |

# LESSON *Planner*

SUBJECT / COURSE:

TOPIC:                                          DATE:

GOAL:                                           LESSON DURATION:

| LESSON OBJECTIVES |
|---|
|  |

| SUMMARY OF TASKS / ACTION PLAN |
|---|
|  |

| MATERIALS / EQUIPMENT |
|---|
|  |

| REFERENCES |
|---|
|  |

| HOME WORK / TASKS |
|---|
|  |

| FEEDBACK |
|---|
|  |

# LESSON *Planner*

SUBJECT / COURSE:

TOPIC:                                                    DATE:

GOAL:                                                     LESSON DURATION:

| LESSON OBJECTIVES |
| --- |
| |

| SUMMARY OF TASKS / ACTION PLAN |
| --- |
| |

| MATERIALS / EQUIPMENT |
| --- |
| |

| REFERENCES |
| --- |
| |

| HOME WORK / TASKS |
| --- |
| |

| FEEDBACK |
| --- |
| |

# LESSON *Planner*

SUBJECT / COURSE:

TOPIC:                                          DATE:

GOAL:                                           LESSON DURATION:

| LESSON OBJECTIVES |
|---|
|  |

| SUMMARY OF TASKS / ACTION PLAN |
|---|
|  |

| MATERIALS / EQUIPMENT |
|---|
|  |

| REFERENCES |
|---|
|  |

| HOME WORK / TASKS |
|---|
|  |

| FEEDBACK |
|---|
|  |

# LESSON *Planner*

SUBJECT / COURSE:

TOPIC:                                          DATE:

GOAL:                                           LESSON DURATION:

| LESSON OBJECTIVES |
| --- |
|  |

| SUMMARY OF TASKS / ACTION PLAN |
| --- |
|  |

| MATERIALS / EQUIPMENT |
| --- |
|  |

| REFERENCES |
| --- |
|  |

| HOME WORK / TASKS |
| --- |
|  |

| FEEDBACK |
| --- |
|  |

# LESSON *Planner*

SUBJECT / COURSE:

TOPIC:

GOAL:

DATE:

LESSON DURATION:

| LESSON OBJECTIVES |
| --- |
|  |

| SUMMARY OF TASKS / ACTION PLAN |
| --- |
|  |

| MATERIALS / EQUIPMENT |
| --- |
|  |

| REFERENCES |
| --- |
|  |

| HOME WORK / TASKS |
| --- |
|  |

| FEEDBACK |
| --- |
|  |

# LESSON *Planner*

SUBJECT / COURSE:

TOPIC:

DATE:

GOAL:

LESSON DURATION:

| LESSON OBJECTIVES |
| --- |
| |

| SUMMARY OF TASKS / ACTION PLAN | MATERIALS / EQUIPMENT |
| --- | --- |
| | |
| | **REFERENCES** |
| | |
| | **HOME WORK / TASKS** |
| | |
| | **FEEDBACK** |
| | |

# LESSON *Planner*

- - - - - - - - - - - - - - - - - - - - - - - - - - - - - - - - - - - - - - - - - - - - - -

SUBJECT / COURSE:

TOPIC:                                                   DATE:

GOAL:                                                    LESSON DURATION:

| LESSON OBJECTIVES |
|---|
|  |

| SUMMARY OF TASKS / ACTION PLAN | MATERIALS / EQUIPMENT |
|---|---|
|  |  |
|  | REFERENCES |
|  |  |
|  | HOME WORK / TASKS |
|  |  |
|  | FEEDBACK |
|  |  |

# LESSON *Planner*

SUBJECT / COURSE:

TOPIC:                                           DATE:

GOAL:                                            LESSON DURATION:

| LESSON OBJECTIVES |
| --- |
| |

| SUMMARY OF TASKS / ACTION PLAN | MATERIALS / EQUIPMENT |
| --- | --- |
| | |
| | **REFERENCES** |
| | |
| | **HOME WORK / TASKS** |
| | |
| | **FEEDBACK** |
| | |

# LESSON *Planner*

SUBJECT / COURSE:

TOPIC:                                    DATE:

GOAL:                                     LESSON DURATION:

| LESSON OBJECTIVES |
| --- |
| |

| SUMMARY OF TASKS / ACTION PLAN | MATERIALS / EQUIPMENT |
| --- | --- |

| REFERENCES |
| --- |

| HOME WORK / TASKS |
| --- |

| FEEDBACK |
| --- |

# LESSON *Planner*

SUBJECT / COURSE:

TOPIC:                                          DATE:

GOAL:                                           LESSON DURATION:

| LESSON OBJECTIVES |
| --- |
|  |

| SUMMARY OF TASKS / ACTION PLAN |
| --- |
|  |

| MATERIALS / EQUIPMENT |
| --- |
|  |

| REFERENCES |
| --- |
|  |

| HOME WORK / TASKS |
| --- |
|  |

| FEEDBACK |
| --- |
|  |

# LESSON *Planner*

- - - - - - - - - - - - - - - - - - - - - - - - - - - - - - - - - - - - - - - - - -

SUBJECT / COURSE:

TOPIC:                                                    DATE:

GOAL:                                                     LESSON DURATION:

| LESSON OBJECTIVES |
|---|
|  |

| SUMMARY OF TASKS / ACTION PLAN | MATERIALS / EQUIPMENT |
|---|---|
|  |  |
|  | REFERENCES |
|  |  |
|  | HOME WORK / TASKS |
|  |  |
|  | FEEDBACK |
|  |  |

# LESSON *Planner*

SUBJECT / COURSE:

TOPIC:                                          DATE:

GOAL:                                           LESSON DURATION:

| LESSON OBJECTIVES |
|---|
|  |

| SUMMARY OF TASKS / ACTION PLAN |
|---|
|  |

| MATERIALS / EQUIPMENT |
|---|
|  |

| REFERENCES |
|---|
|  |

| HOME WORK / TASKS |
|---|
|  |

| FEEDBACK |
|---|
|  |

# LESSON *Planner*

SUBJECT / COURSE:

TOPIC:                                          DATE:

GOAL:                                           LESSON DURATION:

| LESSON OBJECTIVES |
| --- |
| |

| SUMMARY OF TASKS / ACTION PLAN |
| --- |
| |

| MATERIALS / EQUIPMENT |
| --- |
| |

| REFERENCES |
| --- |
| |

| HOME WORK / TASKS |
| --- |
| |

| FEEDBACK |
| --- |
| |

# LESSON *Planner*

- - - - - - - - - - - - - - - - - - - - - - - - - - - - - - - - - - - - - - - - - - - -

**SUBJECT / COURSE:**

**TOPIC:**                                                    **DATE:**

**GOAL:**                                                     **LESSON DURATION:**

| LESSON OBJECTIVES |
|---|
|  |

| SUMMARY OF TASKS / ACTION PLAN |
|---|
|  |

| MATERIALS / EQUIPMENT |
|---|
|  |

| REFERENCES |
|---|
|  |

| HOME WORK / TASKS |
|---|
|  |

| FEEDBACK |
|---|
|  |

# LESSON *Planner*

SUBJECT / COURSE:

TOPIC:                                                DATE:

GOAL:                                                 LESSON DURATION:

| LESSON OBJECTIVES |
|---|
|  |

| SUMMARY OF TASKS / ACTION PLAN |
|---|
|  |

| MATERIALS / EQUIPMENT |
|---|
|  |

| REFERENCES |
|---|
|  |

| HOME WORK / TASKS |
|---|
|  |

| FEEDBACK |
|---|
|  |

# LESSON *Planner*

SUBJECT / COURSE:

TOPIC:

DATE:

GOAL:

LESSON DURATION:

## LESSON OBJECTIVES

## SUMMARY OF TASKS / ACTION PLAN

## MATERIALS / EQUIPMENT

## REFERENCES

## HOME WORK / TASKS

## FEEDBACK

# LESSON *Planner*

SUBJECT / COURSE:

TOPIC:                                          DATE:

GOAL:                                           LESSON DURATION:

| LESSON OBJECTIVES |
| --- |
| |

| SUMMARY OF TASKS / ACTION PLAN |
| --- |
| |

| MATERIALS / EQUIPMENT |
| --- |
| |

| REFERENCES |
| --- |
| |

| HOME WORK / TASKS |
| --- |
| |

| FEEDBACK |
| --- |
| |

# LESSON *Planner*

SUBJECT / COURSE:

TOPIC:                                      DATE:

GOAL:                                       LESSON DURATION:

## LESSON OBJECTIVES

## SUMMARY OF TASKS / ACTION PLAN

## MATERIALS / EQUIPMENT

## REFERENCES

## HOME WORK / TASKS

## FEEDBACK

# LESSON *Planner*

SUBJECT / COURSE:

TOPIC:                                          DATE:

GOAL:                                           LESSON DURATION:

| LESSON OBJECTIVES |
|---|
|  |

| SUMMARY OF TASKS / ACTION PLAN |
|---|
|  |

| MATERIALS / EQUIPMENT |
|---|
|  |

| REFERENCES |
|---|
|  |

| HOME WORK / TASKS |
|---|
|  |

| FEEDBACK |
|---|
|  |

# LESSON *Planner*

SUBJECT / COURSE:

TOPIC:                                              DATE:

GOAL:                                               LESSON DURATION:

### LESSON OBJECTIVES

### SUMMARY OF TASKS / ACTION PLAN

### MATERIALS / EQUIPMENT

### REFERENCES

### HOME WORK / TASKS

### FEEDBACK

# LESSON *Planner*

SUBJECT / COURSE:

TOPIC:                                          DATE:

GOAL:                                           LESSON DURATION:

| LESSON OBJECTIVES |
| --- |
|  |

| SUMMARY OF TASKS / ACTION PLAN |
| --- |
|  |

| MATERIALS / EQUIPMENT |
| --- |
|  |

| REFERENCES |
| --- |
|  |

| HOME WORK / TASKS |
| --- |
|  |

| FEEDBACK |
| --- |
|  |

# LESSON *Planner*

SUBJECT / COURSE:

TOPIC:                                           DATE:

GOAL:                                            LESSON DURATION:

| LESSON OBJECTIVES |
| --- |
|  |

| SUMMARY OF TASKS / ACTION PLAN |
| --- |
|  |

| MATERIALS / EQUIPMENT |
| --- |
|  |

| REFERENCES |
| --- |
|  |

| HOME WORK / TASKS |
| --- |
|  |

| FEEDBACK |
| --- |
|  |

# LESSON *Planner*

SUBJECT / COURSE:

TOPIC:                                              DATE:

GOAL:                                               LESSON DURATION:

| LESSON OBJECTIVES |
|---|
|  |

| SUMMARY OF TASKS / ACTION PLAN |
|---|
|  |

| MATERIALS / EQUIPMENT |
|---|
|  |

| REFERENCES |
|---|
|  |

| HOME WORK / TASKS |
|---|
|  |

| FEEDBACK |
|---|
|  |

# LESSON *Planner*

SUBJECT / COURSE:

TOPIC:                                          DATE:

GOAL:                                           LESSON DURATION:

| LESSON OBJECTIVES |
| --- |
|  |

| SUMMARY OF TASKS / ACTION PLAN |
| --- |
|  |

| MATERIALS / EQUIPMENT |
| --- |
|  |

| REFERENCES |
| --- |
|  |

| HOME WORK / TASKS |
| --- |
|  |

| FEEDBACK |
| --- |
|  |

# LESSON *Planner*

SUBJECT / COURSE:

TOPIC:                                                DATE:

GOAL:                                                 LESSON DURATION:

| LESSON OBJECTIVES |
| --- |
|  |

| SUMMARY OF TASKS / ACTION PLAN | MATERIALS / EQUIPMENT |
| --- | --- |
|  |  |
|  | **REFERENCES** |
|  |  |
|  | **HOME WORK / TASKS** |
|  |  |
|  | **FEEDBACK** |
|  |  |

# LESSON *Planner*

SUBJECT / COURSE:

TOPIC:                                          DATE:

GOAL:                                           LESSON DURATION:

| LESSON OBJECTIVES |
| --- |
|  |

| SUMMARY OF TASKS / ACTION PLAN |
| --- |
|  |

| MATERIALS / EQUIPMENT |
| --- |
|  |

| REFERENCES |
| --- |
|  |

| HOME WORK / TASKS |
| --- |
|  |

| FEEDBACK |
| --- |
|  |

# LESSON *Planner*

- - - - - - - - - - - - - - - - - - - - - - - - - - - - - - - - - - - - - - - - - - - -

SUBJECT / COURSE:

TOPIC:                                           DATE:

GOAL:                                            LESSON DURATION:

| LESSON OBJECTIVES |
| --- |
|  |

| SUMMARY OF TASKS / ACTION PLAN |
| --- |
|  |

| MATERIALS / EQUIPMENT |
| --- |
|  |

| REFERENCES |
| --- |
|  |

| HOME WORK / TASKS |
| --- |
|  |

| FEEDBACK |
| --- |
|  |

# LESSON *Planner*

SUBJECT / COURSE:

TOPIC:                                          DATE:

GOAL:                                           LESSON DURATION:

| LESSON OBJECTIVES |
|---|
|  |

| SUMMARY OF TASKS / ACTION PLAN |
|---|
|  |

| MATERIALS / EQUIPMENT |
|---|
|  |

| REFERENCES |
|---|
|  |

| HOME WORK / TASKS |
|---|
|  |

| FEEDBACK |
|---|
|  |

# LESSON *Planner*

SUBJECT / COURSE:

TOPIC:                                          DATE:

GOAL:                                           LESSON DURATION:

| LESSON OBJECTIVES |
| --- |
|  |

| SUMMARY OF TASKS / ACTION PLAN |
| --- |
|  |

| MATERIALS / EQUIPMENT |
| --- |
|  |

| REFERENCES |
| --- |
|  |

| HOME WORK / TASKS |
| --- |
|  |

| FEEDBACK |
| --- |
|  |

# LESSON *Planner*

SUBJECT / COURSE:

TOPIC:                                          DATE:

GOAL:                                           LESSON DURATION:

| LESSON OBJECTIVES |
|---|
|  |

| SUMMARY OF TASKS / ACTION PLAN |
|---|
|  |

| MATERIALS / EQUIPMENT |
|---|
|  |

| REFERENCES |
|---|
|  |

| HOME WORK / TASKS |
|---|
|  |

| FEEDBACK |
|---|
|  |

# LESSON *Planner*

SUBJECT / COURSE:

TOPIC:                                              DATE:

GOAL:                                               LESSON DURATION:

| LESSON OBJECTIVES |
| --- |
|  |

| SUMMARY OF TASKS / ACTION PLAN | MATERIALS / EQUIPMENT |
| --- | --- |
|  |  |
|  | REFERENCES |
|  |  |
|  | HOME WORK / TASKS |
|  |  |
|  | FEEDBACK |
|  |  |

# LESSON *Planner*

SUBJECT / COURSE:

TOPIC:                                          DATE:

GOAL:                                           LESSON DURATION:

## LESSON OBJECTIVES

## SUMMARY OF TASKS / ACTION PLAN

## MATERIALS / EQUIPMENT

## REFERENCES

## HOME WORK / TASKS

## FEEDBACK

# LESSON *Planner*

SUBJECT / COURSE:

TOPIC:                                          DATE:

GOAL:                                           LESSON DURATION:

| LESSON OBJECTIVES |
|---|
|  |

| SUMMARY OF TASKS / ACTION PLAN | MATERIALS / EQUIPMENT |
|---|---|
|  |  |
|  | REFERENCES |
|  |  |
|  | HOME WORK / TASKS |
|  |  |
|  | FEEDBACK |
|  |  |

# LESSON *Planner*

SUBJECT / COURSE:

TOPIC:                                          DATE:

GOAL:                                           LESSON DURATION:

## LESSON OBJECTIVES

## SUMMARY OF TASKS / ACTION PLAN

## MATERIALS / EQUIPMENT

## REFERENCES

## HOME WORK / TASKS

## FEEDBACK

# LESSON *Planner*

SUBJECT / COURSE:

TOPIC:

DATE:

GOAL:

LESSON DURATION:

| LESSON OBJECTIVES |
| --- |
|  |

| SUMMARY OF TASKS / ACTION PLAN |
| --- |
|  |

| MATERIALS / EQUIPMENT |
| --- |
|  |

| REFERENCES |
| --- |
|  |

| HOME WORK / TASKS |
| --- |
|  |

| FEEDBACK |
| --- |
|  |

# LESSON *Planner*

SUBJECT / COURSE:

TOPIC:                                          DATE:

GOAL:                                           LESSON DURATION:

| LESSON OBJECTIVES |
| --- |
| |

| SUMMARY OF TASKS / ACTION PLAN | MATERIALS / EQUIPMENT |
| --- | --- |
| | |
| | **REFERENCES** |
| | |
| | **HOME WORK / TASKS** |
| | |
| | **FEEDBACK** |
| | |

# LESSON *Planner*

SUBJECT / COURSE:

TOPIC:                                         DATE:

GOAL:                                          LESSON DURATION:

| LESSON OBJECTIVES |
|---|
|  |

| SUMMARY OF TASKS / ACTION PLAN | MATERIALS / EQUIPMENT |
|---|---|
|  |  |
|  | **REFERENCES** |
|  |  |
|  | **HOME WORK / TASKS** |
|  |  |
|  | **FEEDBACK** |
|  |  |

# LESSON *Planner*

SUBJECT / COURSE:

TOPIC:                                          DATE:

GOAL:                                           LESSON DURATION:

| LESSON OBJECTIVES |
| --- |
| |

| SUMMARY OF TASKS / ACTION PLAN |
| --- |
| |

| MATERIALS / EQUIPMENT |
| --- |
| |

| REFERENCES |
| --- |
| |

| HOME WORK / TASKS |
| --- |
| |

| FEEDBACK |
| --- |
| |

# LESSON *Planner*

SUBJECT / COURSE:

TOPIC:

GOAL:

DATE:

LESSON DURATION:

| LESSON OBJECTIVES |
| --- |
| |

| SUMMARY OF TASKS / ACTION PLAN |
| --- |
| |

| MATERIALS / EQUIPMENT |
| --- |
| |

| REFERENCES |
| --- |
| |

| HOME WORK / TASKS |
| --- |
| |

| FEEDBACK |
| --- |
| |

# LESSON *Planner*

SUBJECT / COURSE:

TOPIC:                                          DATE:

GOAL:                                           LESSON DURATION:

| LESSON OBJECTIVES |
|---|
|  |

| SUMMARY OF TASKS / ACTION PLAN | MATERIALS / EQUIPMENT |
|---|---|
|  | |
|  | REFERENCES |
|  | |
|  | HOME WORK / TASKS |
|  | |
|  | FEEDBACK |
|  | |

# LESSON *Planner*

SUBJECT / COURSE:

TOPIC:

DATE:

GOAL:

LESSON DURATION:

| LESSON OBJECTIVES |
| --- |
| |

| SUMMARY OF TASKS / ACTION PLAN |
| --- |
| |

| MATERIALS / EQUIPMENT |
| --- |
| |

| REFERENCES |
| --- |
| |

| HOME WORK / TASKS |
| --- |
| |

| FEEDBACK |
| --- |
| |

# LESSON *Planner*

SUBJECT / COURSE:

TOPIC:

GOAL:

DATE:

LESSON DURATION:

| LESSON OBJECTIVES |
|---|
|  |

| SUMMARY OF TASKS / ACTION PLAN | MATERIALS / EQUIPMENT |
|---|---|
|  |  |

REFERENCES

HOME WORK / TASKS

FEEDBACK

# LESSON *Planner*

- - - - - - - - - - - - - - - - - - - - - - - - - - - - - - - - - - - - - - - - - - - - -

SUBJECT / COURSE:

TOPIC:                                                    DATE:

GOAL:                                                     LESSON DURATION:

| LESSON OBJECTIVES |
|---|
|  |

| SUMMARY OF TASKS / ACTION PLAN |
|---|
|  |

| MATERIALS / EQUIPMENT |
|---|
|  |

| REFERENCES |
|---|
|  |

| HOME WORK / TASKS |
|---|
|  |

| FEEDBACK |
|---|
|  |

# LESSON *Planner*

SUBJECT / COURSE:

TOPIC:                                          DATE:

GOAL:                                           LESSON DURATION:

| LESSON OBJECTIVES |
|---|
|  |

| SUMMARY OF TASKS / ACTION PLAN | MATERIALS / EQUIPMENT |
|---|---|
|  |  |
|  | **REFERENCES** |
|  |  |
|  | **HOME WORK / TASKS** |
|  |  |
|  | **FEEDBACK** |
|  |  |

# LESSON *Planner*

SUBJECT / COURSE:

TOPIC:

GOAL:

DATE:

LESSON DURATION:

| LESSON OBJECTIVES |
| --- |
| |

| SUMMARY OF TASKS / ACTION PLAN |
| --- |
| |

| MATERIALS / EQUIPMENT |
| --- |
| |

| REFERENCES |
| --- |
| |

| HOME WORK / TASKS |
| --- |
| |

| FEEDBACK |
| --- |
| |

# LESSON *Planner*

SUBJECT / COURSE:

TOPIC:                                    DATE:

GOAL:                                     LESSON DURATION:

| LESSON OBJECTIVES |
|---|
|  |

| SUMMARY OF TASKS / ACTION PLAN | MATERIALS / EQUIPMENT |
|---|---|
|  |  |
|  | **REFERENCES** |
|  |  |
|  | **HOME WORK / TASKS** |
|  |  |
|  | **FEEDBACK** |
|  |  |

# LESSON *Planner*

- - - - - - - - - - - - - - - - - - - - - - - - - - - - - - - - - - - - - - - - - - - - - - -

SUBJECT / COURSE:

TOPIC:                                                    DATE:

GOAL:                                                     LESSON DURATION:

| LESSON OBJECTIVES |
|---|
|  |

| SUMMARY OF TASKS / ACTION PLAN | MATERIALS / EQUIPMENT |
|---|---|
|  | |
|  | **REFERENCES** |
|  | |
|  | **HOME WORK / TASKS** |
|  | |
|  | **FEEDBACK** |
|  | |

# LESSON *Planner*

SUBJECT / COURSE:

TOPIC:                                          DATE:

GOAL:                                           LESSON DURATION:

| LESSON OBJECTIVES |
|---|
|  |

| SUMMARY OF TASKS / ACTION PLAN |
|---|
|  |

| MATERIALS / EQUIPMENT |
|---|
|  |

| REFERENCES |
|---|
|  |

| HOME WORK / TASKS |
|---|
|  |

| FEEDBACK |
|---|
|  |

# LESSON *Planner*

SUBJECT / COURSE:

TOPIC:                                              DATE:

GOAL:                                               LESSON DURATION:

| LESSON OBJECTIVES |
| --- |
|  |

| SUMMARY OF TASKS / ACTION PLAN |
| --- |
|  |

| MATERIALS / EQUIPMENT |
| --- |
|  |

| REFERENCES |
| --- |
|  |

| HOME WORK / TASKS |
| --- |
|  |

| FEEDBACK |
| --- |
|  |

# LESSON *Planner*

SUBJECT / COURSE:

TOPIC:

DATE:

GOAL:

LESSON DURATION:

| LESSON OBJECTIVES |
| --- |
|  |

| SUMMARY OF TASKS / ACTION PLAN | MATERIALS / EQUIPMENT |
| --- | --- |
|  |  |
|  | REFERENCES |
|  |  |
|  | HOME WORK / TASKS |
|  |  |
|  | FEEDBACK |
|  |  |

# LESSON *Planner*

SUBJECT / COURSE:

TOPIC:

GOAL:

DATE:

LESSON DURATION:

| LESSON OBJECTIVES |
|---|
| |

| SUMMARY OF TASKS / ACTION PLAN |
|---|
| |

| MATERIALS / EQUIPMENT |
|---|
| |

| REFERENCES |
|---|
| |

| HOME WORK / TASKS |
|---|
| |

| FEEDBACK |
|---|
| |

# LESSON *Planner*

SUBJECT / COURSE:

TOPIC:                                      DATE:

GOAL:                                       LESSON DURATION:

| LESSON OBJECTIVES |
|---|
|  |

| SUMMARY OF TASKS / ACTION PLAN | MATERIALS / EQUIPMENT |
|---|---|
|  |  |

| REFERENCES |
|---|
|  |

| HOME WORK / TASKS |
|---|
|  |

| FEEDBACK |
|---|
|  |

# LESSON *Planner*

SUBJECT / COURSE:

TOPIC:

GOAL:

DATE:

LESSON DURATION:

| LESSON OBJECTIVES |
| --- |
| |

| SUMMARY OF TASKS / ACTION PLAN |
| --- |
| |

| MATERIALS / EQUIPMENT |
| --- |
| |

| REFERENCES |
| --- |
| |

| HOME WORK / TASKS |
| --- |
| |

| FEEDBACK |
| --- |
| |

# LESSON *Planner*

SUBJECT / COURSE:

TOPIC:                                          DATE:

GOAL:                                           LESSON DURATION:

| LESSON OBJECTIVES |
| --- |
|  |

| SUMMARY OF TASKS / ACTION PLAN |
| --- |
|  |

| MATERIALS / EQUIPMENT |
| --- |
|  |

| REFERENCES |
| --- |
|  |

| HOME WORK / TASKS |
| --- |
|  |

| FEEDBACK |
| --- |
|  |

# LESSON *Planner*

SUBJECT / COURSE:

TOPIC:

DATE:

GOAL:

LESSON DURATION:

| LESSON OBJECTIVES |
|:---:|
|  |

| SUMMARY OF TASKS / ACTION PLAN | MATERIALS / EQUIPMENT |
|:---:|:---:|
|  |  |
|  | REFERENCES |
|  |  |
|  | HOME WORK / TASKS |
|  |  |
|  | FEEDBACK |
|  |  |

# LESSON *Planner*

SUBJECT / COURSE:

TOPIC:

GOAL:

DATE:

LESSON DURATION:

| LESSON OBJECTIVES |
|---|
|  |

| SUMMARY OF TASKS / ACTION PLAN | MATERIALS / EQUIPMENT |
|---|---|
|  |  |

REFERENCES

HOME WORK / TASKS

FEEDBACK

# LESSON *Planner*

SUBJECT / COURSE:

TOPIC:

GOAL:

DATE:

LESSON DURATION:

| LESSON OBJECTIVES |
| --- |
|  |

| SUMMARY OF TASKS / ACTION PLAN | MATERIALS / EQUIPMENT |
| --- | --- |
|  | |
|  | **REFERENCES** |
|  | **HOME WORK / TASKS** |
|  | **FEEDBACK** |

# LESSON *Planner*

SUBJECT / COURSE:

TOPIC:

GOAL:

DATE:

LESSON DURATION:

| LESSON OBJECTIVES |
| --- |
| |

| SUMMARY OF TASKS / ACTION PLAN |
| --- |
| |

| MATERIALS / EQUIPMENT |
| --- |
| |

| REFERENCES |
| --- |
| |

| HOME WORK / TASKS |
| --- |
| |

| FEEDBACK |
| --- |
| |

# LESSON *Planner*

- - - - - - - - - - - - - - - - - - - - - - - - - - - - - - - - - - - - - - - - - - - - - - - - - - - - - - - - - - - - -

SUBJECT / COURSE:

TOPIC:                                                    DATE:

GOAL:                                                     LESSON DURATION:

| LESSON OBJECTIVES |
|---|
|  |

| SUMMARY OF TASKS / ACTION PLAN | MATERIALS / EQUIPMENT |
|---|---|
|  | **MATERIALS / EQUIPMENT** |
|  | **REFERENCES** |
|  | **HOME WORK / TASKS** |
|  | **FEEDBACK** |

# LESSON *Planner*

SUBJECT / COURSE:

TOPIC:                                          DATE:

GOAL:                                           LESSON DURATION:

| LESSON OBJECTIVES |
| --- |
|  |

| SUMMARY OF TASKS / ACTION PLAN |
| --- |
|  |

| MATERIALS / EQUIPMENT |
| --- |
|  |

| REFERENCES |
| --- |
|  |

| HOME WORK / TASKS |
| --- |
|  |

| FEEDBACK |
| --- |
|  |

# LESSON *Planner*

SUBJECT / COURSE:

TOPIC:

GOAL:

DATE:

LESSON DURATION:

| LESSON OBJECTIVES |
|---|
|  |

| SUMMARY OF TASKS / ACTION PLAN |
|---|
|  |

| MATERIALS / EQUIPMENT |
|---|
|  |

| REFERENCES |
|---|
|  |

| HOME WORK / TASKS |
|---|
|  |

| FEEDBACK |
|---|
|  |

# LESSON *Planner*

- - - - - - - - - - - - - - - - - - - - - - - - - - - - - - - - - - - - - - - - - - - - - -

SUBJECT / COURSE:

TOPIC:                                          DATE:

GOAL:                                           LESSON DURATION:

| LESSON OBJECTIVES |
| --- |
|  |

| SUMMARY OF TASKS / ACTION PLAN |
| --- |
|  |

| MATERIALS / EQUIPMENT |
| --- |
|  |

| REFERENCES |
| --- |
|  |

| HOME WORK / TASKS |
| --- |
|  |

| FEEDBACK |
| --- |
|  |

# LESSON *Planner*

SUBJECT / COURSE:

TOPIC:

GOAL:

DATE:

LESSON DURATION:

## LESSON OBJECTIVES

## SUMMARY OF TASKS / ACTION PLAN

## MATERIALS / EQUIPMENT

## REFERENCES

## HOME WORK / TASKS

## FEEDBACK

# LESSON *Planner*

SUBJECT / COURSE:

TOPIC:                                            DATE:

GOAL:                                             LESSON DURATION:

| LESSON OBJECTIVES |
| --- |
|  |

| SUMMARY OF TASKS / ACTION PLAN | MATERIALS / EQUIPMENT |
| --- | --- |
|  |  |
|  | REFERENCES |
|  |  |
|  | HOME WORK / TASKS |
|  |  |
|  | FEEDBACK |
|  |  |

# LESSON *Planner*

SUBJECT / COURSE:

TOPIC:

GOAL:

DATE:

LESSON DURATION:

## LESSON OBJECTIVES

## SUMMARY OF TASKS / ACTION PLAN

## MATERIALS / EQUIPMENT

## REFERENCES

## HOME WORK / TASKS

## FEEDBACK

# LESSON *Planner*

SUBJECT / COURSE:

TOPIC:                                          DATE:

GOAL:                                           LESSON DURATION:

| LESSON OBJECTIVES |
| --- |
| |

| SUMMARY OF TASKS / ACTION PLAN | MATERIALS / EQUIPMENT |
| --- | --- |
| | |

| REFERENCES |
| --- |
| |

| HOME WORK / TASKS |
| --- |
| |

| FEEDBACK |
| --- |
| |

# LESSON *Planner*

SUBJECT / COURSE:

TOPIC:                                          DATE:

GOAL:                                           LESSON DURATION:

| LESSON OBJECTIVES |
| --- |
|  |

| SUMMARY OF TASKS / ACTION PLAN |
| --- |
|  |

| MATERIALS / EQUIPMENT |
| --- |
|  |

| REFERENCES |
| --- |
|  |

| HOME WORK / TASKS |
| --- |
|  |

| FEEDBACK |
| --- |
|  |

# LESSON *Planner*

SUBJECT / COURSE:

TOPIC:

GOAL:

DATE:

LESSON DURATION:

| LESSON OBJECTIVES |
|---|
| |

| SUMMARY OF TASKS / ACTION PLAN |
|---|
| |

| MATERIALS / EQUIPMENT |
|---|
| |

| REFERENCES |
|---|
| |

| HOME WORK / TASKS |
|---|
| |

| FEEDBACK |
|---|
| |

# LESSON *Planner*

SUBJECT / COURSE:

TOPIC:                                          DATE:

GOAL:                                           LESSON DURATION:

| LESSON OBJECTIVES |
| --- |
|  |

| SUMMARY OF TASKS / ACTION PLAN |
| --- |
|  |

| MATERIALS / EQUIPMENT |
| --- |
|  |

| REFERENCES |
| --- |
|  |

| HOME WORK / TASKS |
| --- |
|  |

| FEEDBACK |
| --- |
|  |

# LESSON *Planner*

SUBJECT / COURSE:

TOPIC:                                    DATE:

GOAL:                                     LESSON DURATION:

| LESSON OBJECTIVES |
| --- |
| |

| SUMMARY OF TASKS / ACTION PLAN |
| --- |
| |

| MATERIALS / EQUIPMENT |
| --- |
| |

| REFERENCES |
| --- |
| |

| HOME WORK / TASKS |
| --- |
| |

| FEEDBACK |
| --- |
| |

# LESSON *Planner*

SUBJECT / COURSE:

TOPIC:

DATE:

GOAL:

LESSON DURATION:

| LESSON OBJECTIVES |
|---|
|  |

| SUMMARY OF TASKS / ACTION PLAN |
|---|
|  |

| MATERIALS / EQUIPMENT |
|---|
|  |

| REFERENCES |
|---|
|  |

| HOME WORK / TASKS |
|---|
|  |

| FEEDBACK |
|---|
|  |

# LESSON *Planner*

SUBJECT / COURSE:

TOPIC:

GOAL:

DATE:

LESSON DURATION:

| LESSON OBJECTIVES |
|---|
|  |

| SUMMARY OF TASKS / ACTION PLAN |
|---|
|  |

| MATERIALS / EQUIPMENT |
|---|
|  |

| REFERENCES |
|---|
|  |

| HOME WORK / TASKS |
|---|
|  |

| FEEDBACK |
|---|
|  |

# LESSON *Planner*

SUBJECT / COURSE: _____

TOPIC: _____ DATE: _____

GOAL: _____ LESSON DURATION: _____

| LESSON OBJECTIVES |
| --- |
| |

| SUMMARY OF TASKS / ACTION PLAN |
| --- |
| |

| MATERIALS / EQUIPMENT |
| --- |
| |

| REFERENCES |
| --- |
| |

| HOME WORK / TASKS |
| --- |
| |

| FEEDBACK |
| --- |
| |

# LESSON *Planner*

SUBJECT / COURSE:

TOPIC:

GOAL:

DATE:

LESSON DURATION:

## LESSON OBJECTIVES

## SUMMARY OF TASKS / ACTION PLAN

## MATERIALS / EQUIPMENT

## REFERENCES

## HOME WORK / TASKS

## FEEDBACK

# LESSON *Planner*

SUBJECT / COURSE:

TOPIC:                                              DATE:

GOAL:                                               LESSON DURATION:

| LESSON OBJECTIVES |
|---|
|  |

| SUMMARY OF TASKS / ACTION PLAN |
|---|
|  |

| MATERIALS / EQUIPMENT |
|---|
|  |

| REFERENCES |
|---|
|  |

| HOME WORK / TASKS |
|---|
|  |

| FEEDBACK |
|---|
|  |

# LESSON *Planner*

SUBJECT / COURSE:

TOPIC:

DATE:

GOAL:

LESSON DURATION:

## LESSON OBJECTIVES

## SUMMARY OF TASKS / ACTION PLAN

## MATERIALS / EQUIPMENT

## REFERENCES

## HOME WORK / TASKS

## FEEDBACK

# LESSON *Planner*

SUBJECT / COURSE:

TOPIC:                                          DATE:

GOAL:                                           LESSON DURATION:

| LESSON OBJECTIVES |
|---|
|  |

| SUMMARY OF TASKS / ACTION PLAN | MATERIALS / EQUIPMENT |
|---|---|
|  |  |
|  | **REFERENCES** |
|  |  |
|  | **HOME WORK / TASKS** |
|  |  |
|  | **FEEDBACK** |
|  |  |

# LESSON *Planner*

SUBJECT / COURSE:

TOPIC:

GOAL:

DATE:

LESSON DURATION:

| LESSON OBJECTIVES |
| --- |
| |

| SUMMARY OF TASKS / ACTION PLAN |
| --- |
| |

| MATERIALS / EQUIPMENT |
| --- |
| |

| REFERENCES |
| --- |
| |

| HOME WORK / TASKS |
| --- |
| |

| FEEDBACK |
| --- |
| |

# LESSON *Planner*

SUBJECT / COURSE:

TOPIC:

DATE:

GOAL:

LESSON DURATION:

| LESSON OBJECTIVES |
| --- |
|  |

| SUMMARY OF TASKS / ACTION PLAN |
| --- |
|  |

| MATERIALS / EQUIPMENT |
| --- |
|  |

| REFERENCES |
| --- |
|  |

| HOME WORK / TASKS |
| --- |
|  |

| FEEDBACK |
| --- |
|  |

# LESSON *Planner*

SUBJECT / COURSE:

TOPIC:                                          DATE:

GOAL:                                           LESSON DURATION:

| LESSON OBJECTIVES |
| --- |
|  |

| SUMMARY OF TASKS / ACTION PLAN |
| --- |
|  |

| MATERIALS / EQUIPMENT |
| --- |
|  |

| REFERENCES |
| --- |
|  |

| HOME WORK / TASKS |
| --- |
|  |

| FEEDBACK |
| --- |
|  |

# LESSON *Planner*

SUBJECT / COURSE:

TOPIC:

GOAL:

DATE:

LESSON DURATION:

| LESSON OBJECTIVES |
|---|
|  |

| SUMMARY OF TASKS / ACTION PLAN |
|---|
|  |

| MATERIALS / EQUIPMENT |
|---|
|  |

| REFERENCES |
|---|
|  |

| HOME WORK / TASKS |
|---|
|  |

| FEEDBACK |
|---|
|  |

# LESSON *Planner*

SUBJECT / COURSE:

TOPIC:                                          DATE:

GOAL:                                           LESSON DURATION:

| LESSON OBJECTIVES |
| --- |
| |

| SUMMARY OF TASKS / ACTION PLAN |
| --- |
| |

| MATERIALS / EQUIPMENT |
| --- |
| |

| REFERENCES |
| --- |
| |

| HOME WORK / TASKS |
| --- |
| |

| FEEDBACK |
| --- |
| |

# LESSON *Planner*

SUBJECT / COURSE:

TOPIC:

GOAL:

DATE:

LESSON DURATION:

| LESSON OBJECTIVES |
|---|
|  |

| SUMMARY OF TASKS / ACTION PLAN |
|---|
|  |

| MATERIALS / EQUIPMENT |
|---|
|  |

| REFERENCES |
|---|
|  |

| HOME WORK / TASKS |
|---|
|  |

| FEEDBACK |
|---|
|  |

# LESSON *Planner*

SUBJECT / COURSE:

TOPIC:                                                   DATE:

GOAL:                                                    LESSON DURATION:

| LESSON OBJECTIVES |
| --- |
|  |

| SUMMARY OF TASKS / ACTION PLAN | MATERIALS / EQUIPMENT |
| --- | --- |
|  |  |
|  | **REFERENCES** |
|  |  |
|  | **HOME WORK / TASKS** |
|  |  |
|  | **FEEDBACK** |
|  |  |

Made in the USA
Las Vegas, NV
18 January 2025